AC/DC

Hard Rock Band

Heather Miller

REBELS OF ROCK

Enslow Publishers, Inc.
40 Industrial Road
Box 398
Berkeley Heights, NJ 07922
USA

Library of Congress Cataloging-in-Publication Data

Miller, Heather.
    AC/DC : hard rock band/ Heather Miller.
      p. cm. — (Rebels of rock)
    Summary: "A biography of Australian hard rock band AC/DC"—Provided by publisher.
    Includes bibliographical references (p.   ), discography (p.   ), and index.
    ISBN-13: 978-0-7660-3031-2 (library ed.)
    ISBN-10: 0-7660-3031-8 (library ed.)
    1. AC/DC (Musical group)—Juvenile literature. 2. Rock musicians—Australia—Biography—Juvenile literature. I. Title.
    ML3930.A16M55 2009
    782.42166092'2—dc22
    [B]   2007041901

ISBN-13: 978-0-7660-3623-9 (paperback ed.)
ISBN-10: 0-7660-3623-5 (paperback ed.)

Printed in the United States of America

052010 Lake Book Manufacturing, Inc., Melrose Park, IL

10 9 8 7 6 5 4 3 2

Photo Credits: Chris Brown, p. 81; Photo by Chris Capstick/Rex USA, courtesy of Everett Collection, p. 43; George Chin/Redferns, p. 70; Fin Costello/Redferns, p. 15; Everett Collection, pp. 17, 49, 53; Getty Images, p. 45; Bob King/Redferns, pp. 31; Alan Levine, p. 65; London Features International Ltd., p. 21; Michael Ochs Archive/Getty Images, p. 29, 55; Philip Morris, pp. 4, 9, 37, 60; Ebet Roberts/Redferns, p. 74; Chris Walter/Photofeatures/drr.net, p. 67; WireImage, p. 76; WireImage/Getty Images, p. 27.

Cover Photo: Patrick Ford/Redferns. AC/DC in 1996, from left to right: Cliff Williams, Phil Rudd, Brian Johnson, Malcolm Young, and Angus Young.

CONTENTS

In early 1974, AC/DC played in Chequers, a club in Australia.

A NEW YEAR, A NEW BAND

On New Year's Eve 1973, in a small club called Chequers in Sydney, Australia, a band of young men plugged in their guitars for the first time in front of a live audience. The band's high-energy interpretations of songs from popular bands such as the Rolling Stones, Chuck Berry, and the Beatles brought the crowd to its feet. In addition to their great sound, the wild antics and powerfully athletic performance by lead guitarist Angus Young drove the room wild and transformed the audience into the band's first group of die-hard fans. It seemed that everyone at the club that night realized they had experienced something special. The feeling in the room was overwhelming. This was no ordinary, local band. These guys were going someplace. These guys were going to make it big. The band played as 1974 rolled in. Even more exciting, the new year introduced a new band to Australia. That band was AC/DC and it was on its way to conquering the world, leaving everyone in its path thunderstruck.[1]

Not only did the evening make a big impression on the fans, but also the band members were left feeling exhilarated by the events of the night as they absorbed the awesome reaction of the crowd. Dave Evans, lead singer for the band during the New Year's Eve concert, said, "It [the club] was more packed than usual, as it was New Year's Eve and we went on and really rocked the place. It was magic."[2] Angus Young, lead guitarist, described the reaction of the fans when he said, "From the word go it went great. Everyone thought we were a pack of loonies—you know, who's been feeding them kids bananas?"[3]

When AC/DC first started playing together, band members constantly searched for ways to keep audiences interested. Because of their wild energy onstage, some spectators may have thought the members of AC/DC were completely mad. Others may have thought the band loony because of the off-the-wall costumes they once experimented with. Malcolm Young, the band's second lead guitarist, once wore a pilot's uniform while the bass guitarist impersonated a motorcycle policeman. AC/DC was even known for a short time as the band with the drummer who dressed like a

Harlequin clown. The most experimental band member was most certainly Angus Young, as he sampled several superhero personas such as Spider-man, Zorro, and a character similar to Superman: "Super A." While performing as a superhero, Angus would enter a phone both onstage as an ordinary man and emerge from the prop dressed as Super A. The superhero theme was short-lived and ultimately abandoned when the booth's door became stuck and Angus found himself trapped inside the tiny glass room during a performance.[4]

After a round of trial and error with a variety of props and stage clothes, the only costume that stuck was the school uniform worn by Angus. The idea of wearing the uniform was the result of a suggestion made by the Young brothers' sister, Margaret Young.[5] Margaret remembered Angus coming home from school, going straight to his bedroom, and picking up his guitar to play for hours all while still wearing his school uniform. The image stuck in Margaret's mind, and it was she who put together the idea of wearing the uniform onstage.[6] Angus pieced together a uniform that included a typical blazer worn with a white-collared shirt complete with a traditional striped tie. Short trousers showed off his knee-high socks that were almost always worn with one pulled up and the other slouched around his ankle. Angus added a big letter A to the blue cap that tamed his mop of messy hair, something that would have never been allowed at his former private school. The uniform broke just enough rules to give fans a hint of his true rebellious side.[7] When telling about the audience's reaction to the costume, Angus said, "The first thing they saw was me. It was like a cold slap in the face. And they thought, 'Is it a joke?' First reaction was people would sort of giggle. And Malcolm would say to me 'Shut 'em up! You can play.' It was a good thing because they were going to remember us for the little guy in the short pants who looks like he's having an epileptic fit. But the thing is you had to play."[8] The striped tie, blazer, and short pants may have come together as an experimental gimmick, but they have since become an international identifying symbol of the band. And, after more than thirty years of performing, Angus still wears the trademark uniform during live concerts. Anxious fans go wild when Angus takes the stage showing off his knobby knees under his short pants!

Electric Energy

Angus's uniform may have grabbed the attention of the audiences, but it was the band's energy and ability to play music that kept fans coming back for more. The energy spewed out by AC/DC onstage was quickly absorbed by the band's fans. Those attending an AC/DC concert knew they were in for a night of fun and excitement. But what appeared to be a band of players having an amazing time onstage was actually a group of men pouring their hearts into a gig that would barely buy their next meal. In the early days, each concert the band played was viewed as another step to struggle past poverty as

AC/DC EXPERIMENTED WITH DIFFERENT COSTUMES. ONLY ANGUS YOUNG'S SCHOOLBOY UNIFORM HAS STAYED WITH THE BAND THROUGHOUT THE YEARS.

they slowly made their way toward success. They tried their best and put forth as much determination as they could scrape up. Sometimes the frustration built up so much that it exploded onstage. AC/DC was known for blowing up amplifiers and smashing guitars during performances. Fans were thrilled by the raw and authentic display of emotions. When describing his urge for guitar smashing, Angus Young said, "The tensions build up within you and it can go just so far. Then something's gotta give. It's not gonna be me, so the guitar has to be the one."[9] While the act of smashing guitars gave the band an emotional release, it also cost the band a fair amount of money.

Because the band was barely making enough money to buy food, replacing instruments was simply impossible. After a destructive night, broken guitars were put back together and blown-up amplifiers were fixed. But, the violent displays were worth the effort. The shock value of the band's wild behavior increased their fan base and made the band even stronger.

Wild Angus

Many would say that Angus provides the most shock value of them all. Although he dresses in a traditional, conservative English schoolboy uniform, he is nowhere close to being reserved. While performing, Angus often ends up lying on the stage floor, flailing and kicking his legs as if he were being electrocuted, all while his spastic fingers fly up and down the guitar frets in perfect timing with the rest of his bandmates. One newspaper reporter described Angus looking like a "kangaroo hopping, neck out like an emu."[10] Angus's stage antics are now world famous, but their origin was the result of nothing more than a clumsy accident.

Angus gave his account of the story when he said, "One night I tripped up and fell on my knees. When something like that happens, you feel such a fool so I began rolling around on the floor and carrying on in that fashion. It proved to be the only time we got any applause that night."[11] It has been said that in the early days Angus often walked around with bruised knees covered by cuts and gashes.

Besides throwing himself on the floor to delight fans, Angus was known to throw himself into the audience, an act that drove crowds wild and sometimes even frightened them. During today's rock concerts such actions are often expected, but Angus was one of the first to involve fans in this way. He was a young rocker who was definitely considered a cutting-edge performer. So much so that it has been written that one reporter once doubted the authenticity of his performance and accused Angus of playing along with a recording. The reporter cast doubt on Angus by saying no one could possibly flail around the stage so wildly and still manage to play the guitar. All doubt was thrown aside as night after night, concert after concert, Angus continued to wow crowds with his excessive energy and skillful guitar playing. Today there is no question: Angus is consumed by the energy of rock and roll as even now, the middle-aged musician controls the stage with unbelievable energy.[12]

When AC/DC took the stage during the last moments of 1973, their antics shocked most adults but fascinated and electrified Australia's youth. The band's debut left both adults and kids asking, "Who is this band?" The answer is AC/DC, a band who would rock their way to success and find themselves compared to other great classic rockers such as the Rolling Stones and Led Zeppelin. AC/DC had a long road in front of them, but they were well on their way to fame, fortune, and worldwide success.

BAND OF BROTHERS

A C/DC is a band that has gone through many changes. During the past thirty years, nearly twenty different musicians have played as members of the group. Each change in membership brought the group one step closer to the band that exists today. AC/DC's current members include guitarists Malcolm and Angus Young, lead vocalist Brian Johnson, drummer Phil Rudd, and bass guitar player Cliff Williams.

The Young Boys

It has been said that former lead singer Bon Scott's electric personality shot the lightning bolt through AC/DC's name, but no one can argue that it was the Young brothers who laid the foundation for the band. Malcolm Young and Angus Young, two talented lead guitar players, were the first seeds that slowly grew and transformed a group of rock and roll–loving guys from Australia into a band that has withstood the unknown and moved into the millennium as one of the world's most well-known classic rock groups of all time.

The Young household could not be described as a calm, quiet place where children sat in their chairs and ate their peas and carrots peacefully while sitting down at the table for a warm, Sunday meal. It was, however, a family full of energy and creativity. With nine children running about,[1] parents William and Margaret Young turned to music to give the family a creative outlet. The Young family owned a variety of instruments that included a piano, a guitar, a banjo, and a saxophone, with which the children could experiment.

Living in Glasgow, Scotland, in the 1960s, happy, joyous times were hard to come by. The Young family's collection of instruments, as well as their taste in upbeat music, helped them push aside the dreary feelings that often come with a lifestyle of struggle. Glasgow was a dirty and dangerous city. With a rising crime rate, unsuitable housing, and overpopulation, William and Margaret Young decided to pack up their family and not only leave Glasgow, but also bid farewell to Scotland. In 1963, the Youngs immigrated to Sydney, Australia.[2]

Malcolm Young, the older of AC/DC's two Young brothers, was born on January 6, 1953. For him, the move to Australia was a move to a land of promise. Living in Sydney, which at the time was one of the world's most progressive cities, Malcolm's dreams of becoming a rock star could soar as high as he could imagine.[3]

Angus Young, often referred to as the most identifiable member of AC/DC, was born March 13, 1955, two years later than Malcolm. He also arrived in Sydney with ambitions to become a musician.[4] Steve Armstrong, a childhood friend of both Malcolm and Angus, remembers the Young brothers from school as well as their early commitment to the guitar. Armstrong described his account of the Youngs when he said,

> Through the week they would have to do their guitar lessons after school so we didn't see them when school finished, they would go straight home. But at the weekends they would get the bus and come down and hang out with us, it was a pretty large group and they were just two of the boys, it was great. . . . Both [older brother] George and the boys' parents were major influences on their career because they used to say that guitar practice was a *must*. They would have to do homework first and then it would be guitar practice, every night in the week.[5]

Malcolm and Angus attended Sydney's Ashfield Boys High School. Although they attended school, neither brother excelled in it. Malcolm was known to get in fights at school

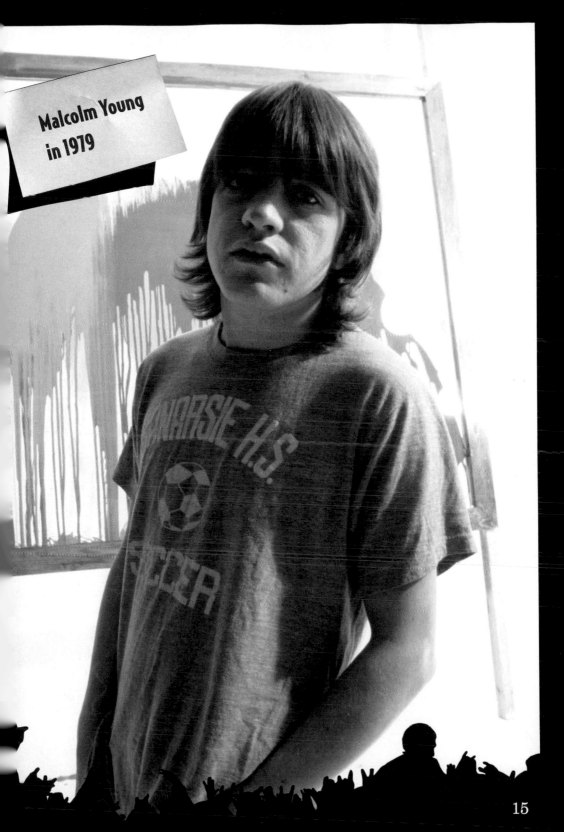

Malcolm Young
in 1979

while teachers labeled Angus as a spunky student who often talked back to authority figures. Inside AC/DC's album *High Voltage*, the text contains an excerpt from a letter that was supposedly written and sent to Malcolm and Angus's mother by Ashfield High's headmaster. The letter read,

> Malcolm is certainly old enough to know that his constant humming is neither amusing nor impressive. The few times a day he puts pen to paper it turns out he is writing what appears to be poetry of some vile sort.
>
> Angus does not stop eating chocolate bars . . . his uniform is filthy, his knees are constantly bruised, his eyes blackened, and his nose running.[6]

Needless to say, Malcolm and Angus stood out as two boys determined to act a bit differently than most teens at Ashfield High. With such restless behavior, it is not a surprise that Malcolm and Angus's taste in music was different from most mainstream adolescents. Rather than turn up the volume to the pop hits of the late 1960s, the Youngs preferred Chicago blues. Angus once said, "I like a lot of the Chicago thing, and a lot of different players. Elmore James, I very much like his style of playing. . . . And B.B. King is another one. Buddy Guy is a great player. And I like Johnny Winter. He's got a lot of power in his blues. . . . For rock and roll I like Chuck Berry's playing. His things are a bit of an art."[7]

Malcolm and Angus's older sister, Margaret, helped plant the love of the blues in the hearts of her brothers. It was she

Angus Young
in 1986

who brought records of Chuck Berry, Fats Domino, and Little Richard into the house. She also brought Malcolm and Angus to see Louis Armstrong, a famous jazz singer and trumpet player, perform live. During an interview, Angus once described the experience of seeing Armstrong when he said, "My sister took me to see him when I was a kid, and I still think he was one of the greatest musicians of all time. Especially when you listen to his old records . . . and hear the incredible musicianship and emotion coming out of his horn."[8]

At age fourteen, academic studies had taken a backseat to music, and Angus dropped out of school just as his brother had done two years before.[9] Angus took a job as a janitor and also worked as a typesetter for a magazine company. Malcolm pulled a paycheck as an apprentice fitter and later as a sewing machine maintenance mechanic. Both boys thought of day jobs as temporary responsibilities as each of them continued to pursue music by playing in his own rock and roll band.[10]

Angus put together the band Tantrum, while Malcolm joined the already established Newcastle, New South Wales group the Velvet Underground.[11] When the Velvet Underground broke up, Malcolm began to look for musicians to form a new band. The new band was none other than AC/DC.

Three in the Lead

In order for AC/DC to become a complete band, it needed a lead singer. Malcolm knew that the lead vocalist would set the tone for the entire band. He was faced with the difficult task of finding a singer with a personality that would give the band the edge it needed to become a success. As Malcolm and the rest of the band members would eventually learn, finding the perfect person to lead the band would prove to be a dramatic adventure filled with success, joy, and tragedy.

Dave Evans

AC/DC's first lead vocalist, Dave Evans, was born on July 20, 1953, to a musical family living in Carmarthen, Wales. His family moved to Australia when Evans was five years old and settled in North Queensland. "I remember arriving in Townsville and thinking how beautiful everything looked from magnificent Castle Hill," Evans once recalled. But beauty was soon lost when the Evans family moved west, to Charters Towers. Evans described his feelings about the move when he said, "It was like going to another planet really. It was hot, dry and brown. I was mortified. I was used to the greenness of Wales and earlier, Townsville. It was a shock."[12] Charters Towers never felt like home to Evans. At seventeen, he was ready for bigger and better things and decided to move to Sydney, Australia, to pursue his musical career.

Although he didn't stay in Charters Towers, he did stick around long enough to form his first band, In Session. The band was the second of only two bands to be heard in Charters Towers. With In Session, Evans brought the first rock and roll band to the small, dry, and brown town. The locals supported the band and, as Evans recalls, "I guess that with the locals telling me how good I was, I suppose I believed them, and knew that if I wanted to make a record that I had to move to where the action was."[13] For Evans, the action would be found in Sydney when he almost stumbled upon the group AC/DC after answering an ad in the newspaper asking for a heavy rock singer.[14]

Bon Scott

Dave Evans may have been the first vocalist for AC/DC, but the lead singer who ultimately kicked the band into high gear was the skinny Scotsman, Ronald Belford Scott. Scott, born July 9, 1946, in Kirriemuir, Scotland, was surrounded by music from the day he came into the world.[15] Scott's parents were music enthusiasts, and their son experimented with several instruments including the piano, accordion, and bagpipes. In the end, it was the drums that spoke to his heart. Scott's mother, Isa, said of her son's musical ability, "Mad on drums, he was, mad on drums. [He] played on a biscuit tin [o]r the bread board . . . People heard him practicing, and they knew."[16] It was evident to many people that Scott had a great deal of musical talent. As a young boy, less than six years old, he joined his father as an active member of the Kirriemuir Pipe Band and together they marched through the town square nearly every Saturday night.[17]

Bon Scott in
the 1970s

When Scott was six years old, his family followed the waves of other Scots who were immigrating to Australia in search of a better life than what they had experienced in Scotland. The Scott family settled in Sunshine, a small community near Melbourne. Scott didn't lose a beat as he accompanied his classmates of Sunshine Primary School on drums as they marched to school every morning.[18] Scott's mother said, "The kids used to march to school and Ron was at the end of the line playing the drums. It kept everybody in step."[19]

Five years after settling in Sunshine, Australia, the Scott family packed up their belongings and moved again. Scott took with him a new nickname, Bonnie, which was given to him by his classmates in honor of his native country "Bonnie Scotland." (Scott later shortened the name to a less feminine version and referred to himself as Bon.) Scott also brought with him his passion for music and drumming, which strengthened as he became a competitive drummer representing John Curtin High and the city of Fremantle, Perth. Scott's performance skills helped him win and hold the title of "under-seventeen champion of Perth" for five years.[20]

Scott's drumming skills offered him several opportunities to show off in front of an audience. Scott and his father performed together during the opening ceremony of the Empire Games in 1962.[21] Being involved in such a large sporting competition was a significant event for the community as well as the Scott family. Scott's brother, Graeme, described his family's pride for the pipe band when he said, "My dad and Ron used to go out to practice for the pipe band, drumming. It was a big occasion when the bands played, the whole family used to go out, put on their kilts, strap the drums on. . . . Those were the big occasions, Scottish things."[22]

Though he enjoyed the traditional sounds of the high school pipe band, the walls of a school building could not contain Scott's rebellious spirit. At fifteen, Scott dropped out of school[23] and tried to earn a few dollars working as a farmhand. When that job didn't work out, he took up the life of a fisherman, then a mechanic's apprentice, and finally a postman. Not surprisingly, Scott's attempts to hold traditional jobs proved to be unsatisfying. It seemed that working by doing the same thing day after day on a strict schedule was not how Scott would satisfy his restless spirit.[24]

Scott's rebellious side began to show its self more and more as he grew older. During a time when conservative citizens considered tattoos taboo, Scott decided to get his first ink when he was a young teen. Choosing to put the tattoo on his lower stomach proved to be an uncomfortable decision, as he had to wear his tight-fitting jeans unzipped for two weeks to help avoid a bit of pain. But the experience must not have been entirely terrible for Scott. As years passed, he added many more tattoos to his collection, including designs on his upper right and left arms as well as his inner left arm.[25]

Tattoos may seem like a drastic form of self-expression to some, but to Scott, they were only a mild form of rebellion. As a teenager, Scott became involved in some serious, risky behavior. More than once, Scott found himself in the middle of street fights, sitting behind the wheel of a stolen car, or siphoning gas from an unattended car.[26]

One particular evening, Scott fell into a bit more trouble than usual when he stepped outside a dance hall to take a walk with a girl. Outside, Scott ended up in the middle of a fight with a group of boys. When the police showed up, Scott dashed off in a friend's car but was soon caught after being spotted trying to steal some gasoline.[27] On March 13, 1963, a local Australian newspaper, the *West Australian*, reported:

> A 16-year-old youth pleaded guilty in the Fremantle Children's Court yesterday to charges of having given a false name and address to the police, having escaped legal custody, having unlawful carnal knowledge and having stolen 12 gallons of petrol.
>
> He was committed to the care of the Child Welfare Department until he was 18 with a recommendation that he be kept in an institution of maximum security.[28]

Scott was taken into custody and sent to the Riverbank boys' home. When his parents arrived, the authorities gave him the choice of being placed back into his parents' custody or serving a nine-month sentence. Scott was so ashamed to face his parents that he chose to fulfill his sentence rather than confront his disappointed mother and father. Even when his grandparents came to visit, Scott refused to see them.[29]

Scott's time spent in juvenile detention, a correction center for youth, was miserable. Riverbank was a cold, dark place designed to hold the most disruptive boys. Scott spent his nights locked in a cell and his days working in the prison laundry and kitchen, scrubbing the floors on his hands and knees.[30]

Scott was released from Riverbank during the Christmas season of 1963. His suffering at the detention center was so great that he vowed he would never return to such a place. Scott straightened himself up and dedicated most of his time and energy to making his dream of joining a rock and roll band come true. He made a bit of money working for the egg board, an organization that controlled the marketing of eggs, and after work, pounded out his frustrations on the drums rather than pounding on other boys. Scott made new friends with a few teens that shared his passion for music. Wyn Milson, John Collins, and Brian Gannon joined forces and put together Scott's first official band, the Spektors.[31]

The Spektors became a popular band on the local scene. Although they were fairly successful, the Spektors combined their talents with another band called the Winztons. Together, they formed a more powerful band and decided to call themselves the Valentines. While playing with the Valentines, Scott began to come out from behind his drums and explore the front of the stage as a singer. Together, Scott and singer Vince Lovegrove shared responsibilities as lead vocalists. Scott would spend half the night as the drummer and then Lovegrove would take over the sticks while Scott brought his talent to the microphone.[32]

In January 1967, a crowd of three thousand teenagers watched as the Valentines stepped in front of the largest group of fans they had ever played for. The response was positive and the band received critical acclaim in the *Sunday Times* when a reporter wrote, "lead singers [Scott] and Vince clearly demonstrated [sic] their vibrant personality."[33] The band's popularity continued to grow. So much so that the band members started earning enough money to quit their day jobs. Scott left his job and enjoyed the life of a rock and roll singer. The Valentines were picked up by the record company Clarion Records and were soon opening for the popular band the Easybeats.[34]

Meeting the members and managers of the Easybeats would later become a turning point in Scott's career. Although he had no idea at the time, his introduction to Easybeats songwriter George Young would prove to be the key that opened the door to his involvement with AC/DC.[35]

Brian Johnson

Scott's influence on the band was strong, but his career was relatively short-lived and sadly ended in tragedy. Following

Brian Johnson
in 1981

the loss of Scott, another Englishman, Brian Johnson, picked up the role of lead singer. Born in Newcastle Upon Tyne, England, on October 5, 1947, Johnson was also a child raised with strong musical influences. As a young boy, Johnson sang in the church choir, but he certainly didn't develop his distinctive hard-rocking voice during Sunday morning services. Johnson started singing with his first significant rock band when he was twenty-five years old. The band was called USA.[36] Not long after USA was formed, the band changed their name to Geordie. It was through his work with Geordie that Johnson's voice really took off. In fact, his voice was so distinctive that a member of AC/DC would remember his performance and suggest that he would serve the band well as the lead singer. Years later, Johnson would answer a phone call from AC/DC's managers asking him to audition with the band.

Phil Rudd Sets the Beat

Drummer Phil Rudd, the only full-blooded Australian in the band, was born in Melbourne on May 19, 1954. With a birth name as long as some sentences, Phillip Hugh Norman Witschke Rudd, nee Redzevecuis, stood out as a drummer with both passion and skill. After his audition for AC/DC in 1975, the band knew they had found the man who would lay the rhythmic foundation for the group. Rudd's ability impressed AC/DC so much that, after hearing him play, the band stopped their search for a new drummer and hired Rudd on the spot.[37]

PHIL RUDD IN 1977

Although he was immediately welcomed by AC/DC, Rudd did not find success without struggle. He made his first bit of money washing cars while drumming for the band Charlemagne. Rudd later hooked up with Colored Balls, a group that did well in Australia's club scene and recorded two singles: "Liberate Rock" and "Mess of Blues." After recording one album with the group of players in Colored Balls, Rudd grew tired of the scene and began to search for a new group to play with. The timing was perfect. Rudd needed AC/DC at the same time the band needed him.[38]

Rudd played with AC/DC from 1975 until 1983, when he found himself in the middle of a heated argument with Malcolm Young. Stories say punches were thrown and within hours, Rudd was thrown out of the band and sent home. An audition was held, and Simon Wright was put behind the drum kit to replace Rudd.

Rudd took up residence in New Zealand where he owned and operated a helicopter business. His absence from the music business lasted over ten years. In 1991, his old bandmates stopped by to visit Rudd after playing a concert in New Zealand. The visit went well and all harsh feelings seemed to be mended. Three years later, in May 1994, AC/DC invited Rudd to a band practice. He conceded and soon after that he was invited to rejoin the band. Today, he continues to play with AC/DC and adds his own spark to the band's highly energetic style.[39]

Cliff Williams

Energetic and motivated bass guitar player Cliff Williams felt such a strong connection to the bass guitar that he taught himself to play. Born in Rumford, England, on December 14, 1949, Williams was destined to grow up with heavy rock and roll influences. At age nine, his family moved to Liverpool, the home of one of history's most famous bands, the Beatles.[40] The Beatles led the rock and roll revolution in England, spearheaded the "British Invasion" that brought a new wave of

Cliff Williams in 1988

music to the United States, and is still considered one of the most commercially successful bands in music history.[41] The overwhelming success of the Beatles sent Liverpool teens into a musical frenzy. For young teens, hooking up with friends to start a band was the thing to do. Williams and his friends were no different. At sixteen, Williams was playing bass well enough to add his sound to his own band.

At first, playing in a band was just something Williams did for fun. He didn't find himself playing seriously until after he worked as an engineer in an office building located behind a rail station in Liverpool. The life of a businessman didn't hold Williams's attention for long. After two years of working in an office, Williams joined a band called Home. In 1970, Home recorded two songs with Epic Records.

In 1971, Williams was given a thrilling opportunity as he was asked to play with the internationally successful band Led Zeppelin during their Electric Magic tour. Little did Williams know that someday he would tour worldwide with his own mega-success band, AC/DC.[42]

AC/DC found Williams after placing an advertisement in *Sounds* magazine. "I got a call from a friend who told me that AC/DC was looking for a bassist and my name was on the list," said Williams.[43] Williams was one of over fifty bass players to audition in a tiny room in Victoria, England. He was asked to play the bass lines for the songs "Live Wire" and "Problem Child." AC/DC members were impressed with his skills, but some reports say that Angus Young chose Williams because he was good-looking and would bring in more female fans. With his good looks and strong guitar skills, Williams became a permanent member of the band on May 27, 1977, and has since played with AC/DC for thirty years.[44]

Balancing the personalities of a motley gang of rebellious teens and molding the playing styles of a group of headstrong rock and roll enthusiasts was no easy task. But after years of battling strong opinions, surviving wild nights of excess, losing old members and gaining new, Malcolm Young and his little brother Angus had finally found the group of men who would forever be remembered as AC/DC.

A SPARK EXPLODES

Without the daily newspaper the *Sydney Morning Herald*, the boys of AC/DC may never have found each other and the band may never have been organized. In his search for band members, Malcolm Young placed an advertisement in the paper calling for a "[heavy] rock singer."[1] Dave Evans responded, and to his surprise, Malcolm picked up the phone. Malcolm and Evans had heard about each other through their experience with their former band, the Velvet Underground. Dave Evans described his account of the conversation when he said in an interview, "I answered an ad in the *Sydney Morning Herald* for a heavy rock singer. When I answered the ad the guy on the other end of the phone said, 'Who is it?' I said, 'Dave Evans,' he said, 'This is Malcolm Young' . . . he said 'I've got two guys here. We've been jamming and we've been looking for a singer to form the band.'"[2] Evans joined the Underground soon after Malcolm left the band, so when the connection was made during the initial phone conversation, Malcolm was excited to meet Evans in person and said, "Hey, get down to Newton, in Sydney here."[3]

Evans, along with two other musicians Malcolm had found, Colin Burgess and Larry Van Kriedt, jammed for the first time in an abandoned office building that had been refashioned into a rehearsal studio.[4] Evans said of the session, "It was good. . . . We all shook hands and said, 'Yes. We have a band.' We didn't have a name but we had a band."[5] Burgess remembers how Malcolm first contacted him, "This guy rang me up and said 'Malcolm Young wants to form a new band.' At the time I didn't even know who Malcolm was . . . we set up a rehearsal and it sounded great."[6]

Van Kriedt had known Malcolm for quite some time. While living in a migrant hostel, Van Kriedt first met Angus when he stopped by the hostel after school to visit some other friends. Van Kriedt said, "The first time I saw him he was wearing a school uniform, carrying an electric guitar and smoking a cigarette. He was 14 or 15. I had a real Gibson guitar and I could play it so we became friends."[7] Angus introduced Van Kriedt to his family, and, being a guitar player, he fit right in. Van Kriedt stopped by the Young house almost every weekend to play guitar with both Angus and Malcolm. After losing touch with the Youngs for a couple of years, Van Kriedt received an invitation from Malcolm to join his new band. Van Kriedt said, "I was probably only in AC/DC for about four months. But it seemed like longer. Everyone could see that it was going somewhere."[8]

Malcolm still thought the band was missing something. The idea of adding a piano to the band was mentioned, but quickly dropped. Angus remembers, "Malcolm didn't want a piano in the band. Rock 'n' Roll's gotta be about gut guitars."[9] A few weeks later, Malcolm asked the other players if his brother Angus could audition. The others agreed and Angus brought another guitar into the mix. Evans said of the addition of Angus to the band, "It sounded good, it sounded great. So there was another one [brother], it was five of us. We still didn't have a name at this stage."[10]

Naming the Band

Surprisingly, it was a sewing machine that ended up giving AC/DC its name. Once again, the Young brothers' sister, Margaret, offered her creative thoughts to the shaping of AC/DC. It was she who noticed the letters "AC/DC" printed on the back of her sewing machine. The reference to electrical power made an impression on Margaret so she suggested it to the band.[11] Evans recalled the band's reaction to her idea when he said, "We really didn't have a name in mind but we talked that we [were] all gonna write three names, put it in the hat, pull it out, and that'll be our name. But on that particular rehearsal, Malcolm said 'look, my sister got a name—AC/DC—what do you think?' We said 'it sounds great, power . . .' that kind of stuff. . . . We didn't end up doing the draw out of the hat, we just went with AC/DC."[12]

Although the original name stayed with the band, few of the original members did. Just months after the band started,

AC/DC IN THE EARLY 1970s WAS, FROM LEFT TO RIGHT: ROB BAILEY, ANGUS YOUNG, MALCOLM YOUNG, DAVE EVANS, AND PETER CLACK.

Van Kriedt was replaced by Rob Bailey on bass. Drummer Colin Burgess was fired after falling out of his drum kit during a live performance. Burgess claims his drink must have been tampered with. He remembers Malcolm saying to him, "You're so drunk you can't play, so you've got the sack." Burgess remembers, "I had to sit down for a while anyway when I came offstage because I was still like jelly. Someone must have spiked my drink or something . . ."[13] Several other drummers flowed in and out of the group before Peter Clack stayed on long enough to record the band's first single, "Can I Sit Next to You Girl?" in 1974.

Early Memories

There were no private jets to escort AC/DC across Australia in the early days. When the band first began playing, they traveled by truck from one side of Australia to the other. The route between Sydney and Melbourne took between twelve and fourteen hours. Another common trip, the route between Adelaide and Perth, Australia, took two days.[14] AC/DC played almost every night at bars and nightclubs all around Australia. They once put on a free concert at the Sydney Opera House and even provided the entertainment for a backyard wedding. The band was determined to make it, and they worked very hard to make their dream of becoming a successful rock band a reality.

As the band began to develop its own style, disagreements

about the band's image started breaking bonds between AC/DC's members. Lead singer Dave Evans wanted the band to follow in the footsteps of other glam rock bands. The Young brothers were completely turned off by the heavy, glittery makeup and space-aged costumes worn by glam rockers such as David Bowie and T-Rex.[15] Instead, they wanted AC/DC to pursue a simpler sound modeled after blues artists Muddy Waters and B. B. King.

During this time of early turmoil, Malcolm and Angus kept an eye out for a new lead singer. A friend of the Young family, Vince Lovegrove, who also managed a few bands in Australia, knew a singer who he thought would fit in perfectly with AC/DC.

Bon Scott, a thirty-three year old who at that time was singing for the band Fraternity, also worked for Lovegrove doing odd jobs. Scott sometimes worked as a driver who transported bands to their gigs. He also worked as a roadie who helped carry and set up equipment for various bands. Ironically, one of the bands that Scott stumbled across was AC/DC. Lovegrove was a fan of both AC/DC and Scott. Lovegrove remembers, "One day Malcolm told me they were going to sack their singer, and he asked me if I knew anyone."[16] When Lovegrove suggested Scott as a possible singer for AC/DC, the boys in the band scowled at the idea, saying Scott was too old and couldn't possibly have the energy they were looking for. When the idea of joining AC/DC was mentioned to Scott, he replied that the band was too young!

Lovegrove was the only person involved with the deal who knew both sides of the story. He was certain that Scott was exactly the type of singer AC/DC was looking for.[17] During the fall of 1974, Lovegrove took Scott to see AC/DC perform in Adelaide, Australia. Scott was thrilled by the band's energy. Scott described the moment when Lovegrove brought him backstage to meet the band when he said, "I took the opportunity to explain to them how much better I was than the drongo they had singing with them. So they gave me a chance to prove it, and there I was."[18] After the concert, Scott was invited to jam with the band. His talent was impressive and AC/DC asked Scott to follow them back to Sydney.

Scott did indeed follow the band back to Sydney, but it was a difficult decision for him. He had to leave his own band, Fraternity, and also his unstable marriage. Scott still had strong feelings for his wife, Irene, but in the end decided that his marriage could not be saved. Vince Lovegrove described the moment when he said, "He just packed his bags. He came around with them in the car, he came around to say goodbye, and he wound down the window and said, Seeya later. And that was that."[19] Scott wasn't made an official member of AC/DC until October of the same year when AC/DC's lead singer, Dave Evans, was kicked out of the band after throwing punches at his manager over a disagreement about money.

Evans recalls, "It became a little heated between the manager and me and a few fists were thrown but I don't think anything connected. Anyway it was broken up quickly but that was the incident that sealed my fate as far as my position with AC/DC was concerned. I had just made an important enemy."[20]

The punches thrown by Evans knocked AC/DC onto a new artistic path. New lead singer Bon Scott, with his unique vocal style, added a dark flavor to the band's sound. AC/DC had accomplished what they wanted. The band had distanced itself far from the glam-rock style that Evans had pulled the band toward. Scott would prove to be the driving force that would later catch the ears of rock and roll fans all over the world.

First Album

Excited by their newly found sound, AC/DC hit the grindstone and set to work. In November 1974, the band went into the recording studio to work on their first full-length album. Ten days later they were finished. The album, titled *High Voltage*, included the songs "Baby, Please Don't Go," "Stick Around," and "Show Business" on the Australian version.[21] One story says that while recording, Angus Young's amplifier popped and then started smoking. Even so, the band's manager signaled for the band to continue singing. Some say the incident partly inspired the name of the album. *High Voltage*'s cover was illustrated with a drawing of an electrical substation behind a fence of barbed wire, complete with a dog lifting its leg to piddle.[22]

Interestingly, the song titled "High Voltage" was not included on the album *High Voltage*. The title of the album inspired the band to write a song with the same name. Because the song was not complete at the time the album was released, a single record had to be released for the song. Even without the song "High Voltage," the album was a big hit with Australian fans. Producer Chris Gilbey once commented, "The single became a big hit. The album went on to become an even bigger hit without the song, 'High Voltage' on it! And by the time we had sold a load of albums we were ready to release the next full-length, which did have the song on it, but of course had a different name and that second album was an instant hit. Amazing stuff!"[23] *High Voltage* was an album with a confusing, but successful story.

More Changes

While recording *High Voltage*, Malcolm and Angus Young continued to be frustrated with the overall sound of the band. They felt the rhythm section, which included both bass guitar and drums, was unstable. As a result, two new musicians were brought in—Phil Rudd on drums and Mark Evans (unrelated to former vocalist Dave Evans) on bass guitar.[24] With a solid group of musicians finally found, AC/DC was ready to rock the world.

AFTER A LINEUP CHANGE IN 1974, THE NEW AC/DC CONSISTED OF, FROM LEFT TO RIGHT: BON SCOTT, MARK EVANS, ANGUS YOUNG, PHILIP RUDD, AND MALCOLM YOUNG.

Soon after the addition of Rudd and Evans, in March 1974, AC/DC made their first television performance on a show called *Countdown*. Angus wore his "Super A" costume while the band played "Baby, Please Don't Go." One month later, the band appeared on the show for a second time. This time Angus wore his trademark schoolboy uniform while Scott took the stage wearing a wig of blonde braids, a dress, make-up, and earrings.[25] The idea of a man dressing like a female on television was quite upsetting to a great number of viewers.

Mark Evans remembers the moment by saying, "As soon as his vocals are about to begin he comes out from behind the drums dressed as this schoolgirl. And it was like a bomb went off in the joint; it was pandemonium, everybody broke out in laughter. [Scott] had a wonderful sense of humor."[26] The controversial performance brought a great deal of attention to the band. Australia's youth loved the rebellious attitude of AC/DC. The more the band pushed the limits, the more popular they became. Increased record sales followed and by June, *High Voltage* had been certified gold in Australia.

AC/DC's fans multiplied. Crowds at concerts grew larger. In March 1975, AC/DC played to a crowd of more than twenty-five hundred people at the Myer Music Bowl. Although other bands were scheduled to play at the same concert, after AC/DC's performance a large percentage of the audience left. They had no interest in seeing anyone other than AC/DC.[27] Several months later, a series of free concerts was canceled due to the unruliness of the crowds. More than five thousand AC/DC fans packed Melbourne's Myer Department Store, waiting for the band to arrive. The show was stopped after only two songs as the crowd was simply too large and officials worried about the security of the store.[28]

With a dedicated fan base waiting for new material, AC/DC released its second album in Australia, *T.N.T.*, in late 1975. The album opened with "It's a Long Way to the Top (If You Wanna Rock 'n' Roll)." The song featured Scott on the

IN 1977, AC/DC PERFORMED IN HOLLYWOOD, CALIFORNIA.

bagpipes. Other hits on the album included "Live Wire" and "T.N.T."[29] *T.N.T.* sold more than a hundred thousand copies in Australia, making AC/DC the most successful rock and roll band in the country.[30]

The band had conquered Australia, but still they were not satisfied. Their next battle would be fought in the United Kingdom and then finally the United States. AC/DC was determined to climb the long way to the top of the music industry.

THE WORLD AROUND AC/DC

AC/DC was created by the sons of hardworking fathers. They were teenage boys who skipped school to practice their guitars. They were boys raised without fancy cars or designer clothes. The rebellious souls who put together AC/DC ate simple meals and wore the outgrown clothes of their older brothers. They were a reflection of the working class from which they came, products of the blue-collar neighborhoods in which they lived, and they put together a band that played to the hearts of youth of the everyday man. The music they played was based on a type of music that was born from the souls of hardworking men. That music is called the blues.

Blues Influence

The relaxed, earthy style of the music called the blues came directly from the hearts of hardworking men with troubled souls. The blues most likely originated in the mid-1800s,[1] during a time when the United States was working hard to grow and gain strength as a powerful nation. Agriculture was an important industry and many workers were needed to help with hard, manual labor. Much of the country's labor force came from slavery. African Americans were forced to live as slaves who worked for their owners in the southern United States. While working in the fields, a lead slave worker would call out rhythmic chants that were repeated by the other workers. The steady beat of the music set the pace for their work and also gave the men and women an emotional outlet as they sang about the hardships they were forced to endure.[2] The addition of instruments such as the guitar, drums, harmonica, and bass, combined with songs based on field chants, rounded out the early blues sound.[3]

The lyrics of many blues songs often include unusual phrases or words. For instance, the word "mojo" found in the phrase "got my mojo working," which is often included in blues lyrics, refers to a magic spell, hex, or charm used to bring bad luck to someone else. "Hoochie coochie man" is a phrase that refers to a person who preaches voodoo, a type of folk magic practiced in Haiti and derived from African religion. Phrases made up to describe hard living conditions are also common in blues songs. "Cold in hand" means having no money while "dry so long" refers to being poor.[4] The song "The Blues Had a Baby and They Called It Rock and Roll," sung by Muddy Waters, contains lyrics that explain how rock and roll grew out of a foundation created by the blues.[5]

Early Rock and Roll

In the 1950s, when the members of AC/DC were growing up, the blues sound was picked up by young musicians who made it their own. The new sound was called rock and roll. With its roots steeped in jazz and the blues, rock and roll was thought of as a rebellious expression. Records were shunned by many adults but devoured by the young. Icons such as Elvis Presley and Chuck Berry are examples of musicians who twisted and turned the blues style and created the early sounds of rock and roll.[6]

By today's standards, 1950s rock is often described as having a light sound. Bands made up of clean-cut musicians dressed in matching suits played songs with titles like "Tutti Frutti" and "Rock Around the Clock" to young, screaming fans while disapproving adults stood by and criticized the whole rock and roll movement. The style of this early rock and roll did not appeal to Angus and Malcolm Young as much as the raw sound of the blues, but they did take notice of the rebellious nature of the music.

CHUCK BERRY IS CONSIDERED ONE OF THE PIONEERS OF EARLY AMERICAN ROCK AND ROLL.

Rock and roll's popularity spread quickly with the help of television and radio. As television took over radio's role of offering drama and comedy to the public, radio began to offer more music to its listeners. As more and more radio stations began to play rock and roll songs, the popularity of the genre spread faster and faster.[7] As the music's popularity spread, the music industry's profits began to increase. Record companies motivated by the new wave of money began to control musicians and dictate the music style they could play. With the main goal being to sell records, much of the creativity and rebellion of rock and roll was filtered out by record producers. Rock and roll began to sound softer and smoother until it was whittled down to nothing more than pop music.[8]

In the 1960s, musicians such as Frankie Avalon and Pat Boone, both famous for their smooth, pop-sounding versions of rock and roll, were pushed aside by a booming new force in music: the British Invasion. The British Invasion, led by the Beatles, the Rolling Stones, and the Animals, brought forth a sound that was much more appealing to Angus and Malcolm. These bands brought back the loud, edgy sound of rock and roll that was erased by United States record companies. The British Invasion swept the world, opening new doors for young bands from Britain and beyond.[9]

As the 1960s progressed, rock and roll became louder and louder, which was just perfect for the boys of AC/DC. As the teenagers who would soon become AC/DC banged away at their guitars in their bedrooms and garages, the music they were listening to on the radio kept getting louder and crazier. By the end of the 1960s and into the early 1970s, a new category was added to the rock and roll genre. The new music was called heavy metal or hard rock—the perfect niche for AC/DC. Heavy metal, being more guitar based than early rock and roll, was very similar to the type of music AC/DC was beginning to play. The change helped AC/DC find their place in the music industry. Record companies were looking for bands that played hard rock, and AC/DC was ready to deliver the new sound.

Simple Lyrics

AC/DC's method of creating new songs was very basic. The simple rhythm of the blues sparked ideas for raw, uncluttered music. Nothing fancy went into the process of creating new songs. According to Malcolm Young, the band would make up a riff, or short melody, and the producers would help them turn it into a song. Malcolm once explained the band's care-free style in creating music when he said, "Back then we never went into the studio with anything more than a riff. In fact, we thought a riff was a song. Fortunately, we had the producers there to turn them into songs and it's been pretty much the same ever since. Back then we really didn't know any better."[10] AC/DC's attitude toward creating music is not surprising as their foundation was built on nothing but the basics: plain and raw rock and roll.

Just as the process of creating melody was simple, the band also followed the styling of blues artists when writing lyrics. The words of AC/DC's music were simple and to the point and stemmed from their way of living life to the extreme. Scott, who wrote the lyrics to some of the band's classic tunes such as "Long Way to the Top," a song that describes the band's struggle to success, and "Let There Be Rock," which tells about the creation of rock and roll, pushed the limits of even a rock star's crazy lifestyle to the edge. Scott was no stranger to drugs and alcohol. The words to AC/DC's songs often included detailed descriptions of their experiences with women, drugs, alcohol, and the combination of all three. Critics say Scott's lengthy descriptions of drug use and unclean living carried over into his fans' lives and increased drug use among the youth. Only the young fans that bought records and attended AC/DC concerts can say whether the critics' claims are true or exaggerated.[11]

1970s

AC/DC's lyrics reflected the attitude of the 1970s. After a decade of turmoil in the 1960s, the 70s brought with it a focus on personal pleasures.[12] During the 1960s much of the world experienced social unrest. With the controversial Vietnam War dragging to an end in the early 1970s, many people were simply tired of the stress of war and were anxious to feel good again.

In the shadow of the 1960s when social activism spurred activities such as war protests, the 1970s brought with it a social shift toward a more individualized, self-centered, pleasure-seeking lifestyle.[13]

1980s Hair Bands

The trend of self-indulgence continued into the next decade. In the 1980s, a new generation of hard rock bands flooded the industry. Described as "hair bands," members of groups like Twisted Sister, Poison, and Mötley Crüe stormed the stage wearing heavy makeup and tight, colorful costumes while sporting hairstyles shaped by skillful applications of hairspray. Their decadent style emphasized the essence of the 1980s— excess. Along with musicians, rock stage shows illustrated the extravagant attitude of the era. Flames and fireworks highlighted bands onstage. Musicians were sometimes lowered onto the stage by elaborate pulley and cable systems. While AC/DC did not follow the trend of wearing makeup or ultra-stylized hairdos, they did put on an elaborate stage show.

IN THE 1980s, MUSIC TOOK A TURN IN A DIFFERENT DIRECTION. "HAIR BANDS" SUCH AS POISON WERE POPULAR.

Elaborate props such as cannons and a huge bell were used to add drama to some of the band's biggest hits.

As the 1980s progressed, record producers began to interfere with musicianship as they groomed bands to play a more commercial sound. Bands like Def Leppard and Whitesnake are often accused of "giving in" to the system as they compromised their style with the hopes of making more money. Some music critics claim the rock sound of the late 1980s was teetering on the edge of pop as it began to sound more and more polished and fabricated.

AC/DC was also affected by the literal slowdown in rock. On the album *For Those About to Rock*, tempos were slowed, lyrics were trendy, and the overall sound of the album was often classified as having an "arena rock," or commercial sound. Malcolm Young once gave his opinion of the album when he said, "By the time we'd completed the album, I don't think anyone, neither the band or the producer, could tell whether it sounded right or wrong. Everyone was fed up with the whole album."[14] Luckily, the band did not give in to the influences of their producers for long. By the time the band was ready to record *Flick of the Switch*, they had moved back to their old production team. Tempos on the album were fast, the sound was raw, and once again, fans were happy. While many other hard rock bands were giving in to the pressure from record companies to create a more manufactured, commercial sound, AC/DC knew it was best to stick with their original sound. Record producer Tony Platt once said, *"For Those About To Rock was a bit over-produced in terms of what the band were about. There was a genuine desire to get back to the basics with Flick Of The Switch."*[15] Thanks to past lessons learned, AC/DC still pumps out a sound that is very similar to the style that the earliest fans were drawn to. AC/DC is a band that has stood up to the many changing trends in music. With its roots deeply embedded in the blues, the band has proved that a simple sound is oftentimes the best sound.

ANGUS YOUNG ON THE SHOULDERS OF BON SCOTT DURING A CONCERT IN EARLY 1980.

LIFE AFTER SCOTT

B y 1976, AC/DC had progressed beyond their experimental phase of wearing superhero costumes. They were a solid band made up of members with similar goals and musical styles. AC/DC was still a new group, but with an established foundation, its members were ready to make their appearance on the world music stage.

In 1976, AC/DC signed a contract with the huge recording company Atlantic Records. The new record deal included a touring schedule that sent AC/DC all over Europe. One of AC/DC's first assignments was to serve as the opening band for another band called Back Street Crawler.[1] During a concert, the opening band plays for the crowd as fans wait for the featured act to take the stage. In most cases, the opening band is not as popular as the featured band and fans often give little attention to the unknown group. But for AC/DC, the response was not typical. Back Street Crawler was an older band that was starting to fade. In contrast, AC/DC was a new band, full of energy, and the fans took notice. AC/DC's raw, simple sound won over the crowds. Soon, Back Street Crawler was taking the backseat as AC/DC earned thousands of new fans.[2] Soon after, AC/DC performed as the feature band as they promoted the Lock Up Your Daughters tour. Rather than using an opening band to warm up the fans, AC/DC opened the show with a large-screen video presentation of major artists. The tour also included a contest for fans to participate in. The "Best-dressed Schoolboy or Schoolgirl" competition invited fans to dress like AC/DC band member Angus Young with his long socks, sneakers, and school uniform. The winner of the contest received a new Epiphone Caballero guitar.

The video screen and contest may have been fun gimmicks used to promote and develop excitement over AC/DC, but the band soon proved that contests were not required to tempt fans to fill the seats. Show after show, AC/DC's popularity grew.

First Worldwide Record

To feed the fans' desire for more music from the band, Atlantic Records released AC/DC's first worldwide record. The album was titled *High Voltage*, but it was not the same as the original album by the same name. The worldwide release of *High Voltage* was a collection of the best songs from the Australian album releases *High Voltage* and *T.N.T. Let There Be Rock*, recorded in 1977, followed *High Voltage*. Few would argue the success of *Let There Be Rock*, with recorded sales of 2 million copies. But ultimately, *High Voltage* proved to be more successful with sales reaching 3 million.

The year 1977 may have been successful for album sales, but it also brought with it another significant change. After the recording of *Let There Be Rock*, bassist Mark Evans was asked to leave AC/DC due to increased creative differences between himself and Malcolm Young. Evans was replaced by current AC/DC bassist Cliff Williams.

With successful album sales, the band was ready to try their show on fans across the Atlantic Ocean. On August 16, 1977, writer Susan Masino witnessed AC/DC live for the first time in a small club called the Stone Hearth in Madison, Wisconsin.[3] Masino described her first experience hearing the band when she wrote, "Their sound took on an unearthly volume. [Scott] was standing on the edge of the stage dressed in tight blue jeans, with no shirt on. He looked up into the spotlight and started to scream . . . 'Well if you're lookin' for trouble, I'm the man to see . . .' For the next hour or so, we stood mesmerized by the band." Masino shared the crowd's reaction to the new band by saying, "There weren't that many people in the club, but I do believe every single one of them went upstairs to the loft to meet AC/DC." After the show Masino told the band, "Someday you're going to be as big as the Rolling Stones."[4] Little did Masino know that AC/DC would later go on to tour with the Stones, not as an opening band, but as a double-feature headliner.[5]

The Band Faces Tragedy

By the way things were starting to take off, it may have seemed to the members of AC/DC that their road to the top would be clear and fast. But sadly, that would not be the case. AC/DC was about to endure a terrible tragedy that would change the face of the band forever.

Bon Scott, the leader of the band who captured the hearts of young female fans with his wild, flirtatious eyes, lived a life just as wild as his onstage performances. Although Scott was usually very easy to get along with, he started to show signs of change. Mark Evans described Scott's likeable personality when he said, "He [Scott] was really a pretty mild mannered sort of guy. I mean, I never saw him lose his temper. . . . You could hit him over the head with a baseball bat, and he'd just say, Hey, what are you doing?"[6] But his friends also said that if a person were to pick on one of Scott's girlfriends, they were in for trouble. Once, when leaving a club on a night during which a man had been picking on the band, the same man pulled on Scott's girlfriend's ponytail. Scott went crazy with

BON SCOTT'S LAST PERFORMANCE WITH AC/DC WAS IN 1979.

rage and followed the man outside and beat him with his fists until, as witnesses describe, the man was within an inch of his life.

Scott began to drink more and more alcohol. It was definitely a big part of his lifestyle. Molly Meldrum, an old friend of the band's and reporter for *TV Week*, said, "[Scott] was certainly drinking a lot. Because it was just part of rock'n'roll, it was part of getting to the next gig, doing the gig . . . [Scott] would be there, and he would have his bottle of whisky."[7]

Another of Scott's female friends known as Silver said, "He was drinking a bottle of Scotch a day, even back in those early days of success. I mean, what he was getting in wages wouldn't have covered his Scotch bill."[8] The people that surrounded Scott began to notice him slipping into a lifestyle that included self-destructive amounts of alcohol. Even though night after night swarms of adoring fans cheered him, Scott felt lonely. He longed for someone he could connect with deeply, but with his crazy lifestyle, Scott couldn't find a woman who would devote herself to him. The numb feeling Scott received from drinking large quantities of alcohol made his sadness feel less hurtful. Those who cared about him began to worry.

Silver described her feelings when she said, "I couldn't deal with seeing this incredible, together, really wonderful person that half the world was in love with, and then [after drinking] seeing this dribbling mess that you could have no respect for. . . . [H]e wasn't aggressive, he was just unmanageable. He wouldn't know what city he was in, he'd just lose it."[9]

Scott's drinking habits continued to spiral out of control. He turned to alcohol to drown his sorrows more frequently. Although some stories say that by 1980, Scott was trying to slow down and lead a bit more of a conservative lifestyle, his actions would prove to be self-destructive. On February 19, 1980, Scott worked on writing lyrics for the band's next album. He worked at his apartment, alone, drinking and becoming restless as the night went on.[10] With the urge to go out to a club, Scott called some friends to see if anyone else wanted to join him. While on the phone with his longtime friend Silver, she suggested Scott go out with a mutual friend and fellow musician, Alistair Kinnear.[11] According to reports, Kinnear picked Scott up at his apartment and the pair of them headed to a club called the Music Machine.[12] Kinnear said of the evening, "[Scott] was pretty drunk when I picked him up [at his apartment]. When we got [to the club] there, he was drinking four whiskies straight in a glass at a time."[13] The heavy amounts of alcohol affected both Kinnear and Scott physically. They both became quite drunk and decided to leave the club at about 3:00 A.M.[14] When they arrived at Scott's apartment, Kinnear found Scott's keys and opened the passed-out rocker's apartment, but no one was home. Feeling uncomfortable with leaving Scott alone, Kinnear decided to bring his friend back to his own apartment.[15] When they arrived there, Scott was completely blacked out. Kinnear called Silver to ask her what he should do with Scott. When she answered the phone, Silver said, "Just take some blankets down to him. . . . Leave a note for him, saying which flat's yours, so when he comes to, he can come up."[16]

That night the air was bitter cold. Scott did not wake up

and find his way to Kinnear's apartment. It wasn't until later the next evening, after Kinnear had awakened from his own fifteen-hour alcohol-induced blackout, that he finally ventured down to his car to check on Scott.[17] At 7:45 P.M., Tuesday evening, Kinnear looked in the car and found Scott in the same position as he had left him the night before.[18] Realizing something was seriously wrong, Kinnear drove Scott to King's College Hospital in Denmark Hill.[19] Not knowing how to get in touch with Scott's parents, Kinnear gave the hospital Silver's phone number.

Silver rushed to the hospital. She described the events when she said, "I went down there with Joe (a friend). Joe had worked in hospitals. They didn't tell me he was dead. They told me he was there, and it was serious . . . we got shown into a little room . . . it was a bit of a surprise being put into this little room. And then they brought us a cup of tea, and Joe said, Look, this isn't right. They don't do this, he must be dead, they're going to send a doctor in to tell us."[20] Sadly, Joe was right. Soon a doctor came in to share the horrible news. Scott's death certificate describes the circumstances in very direct words: "Ronald Belford Scott, Cause of death: Acute alcoholic poisoning, Death by Misadventure."[21]

Most stories say Angus was the first bandmate to receive the news. Reports say he received a phone message from Silver saying that Scott had been rushed to the hospital and was pronounced dead.[22] Angus relayed the message to his brother Malcolm who in turn called Scott's family.

Scott's sudden death was hard for his fellow band members to accept. At first they thought there had been a misunderstanding or that it was simply a rumor. Malcolm described the loss as painful as losing a member of one's own family. "Maybe even a bit worse, 'cos we all had a lot of respect for [Scott] as a person," said Malcolm.[23]

Although his death was a surprise, it was not a complete shock to those that knew Scott well. Scott himself once told ex-manager Michael Browning that he would die a young man. "[Scott] always used to say that he was pretty sure he wouldn't live beyond 40. So I think in some ways everybody kind of expected it to happen if he was left to his own devices," said Browning.[24]

The funeral was kept quiet. The arrangements were not announced to the public, and as a result, the family was able to pay their last respects to their son without intrusive cameras or reporters asking personal questions. The band members came to the services, but few others from the music industry attended.

The funeral wasn't the last time those close to him would think of Scott. A few weeks after the services, friends and family began receiving Christmas cards from Scott. Apparently Scott put his cards in the mail without appropriate postage, putting a delay on their delivery. Much to their surprise, those

In Fremantle Cemetery in Australia, people may pay their respects to Bon Scott at this memorial. It has been reported that hundreds of people each year visit the site.

people closest to Scott received a final message from him in their mailboxes—a final note of good tidings from a man who had served many people as a true friend.[25]

Twenty years later, the anniversary of Scott's death prompted many people working in the music industry to reflect on Scott's life. Music critic Bruce Elder described his feelings about Scott when he said,

> I guess the important thing about Bon Scott was that he was a genuinely larger than life character and he is remembered as that with great affection. I think that every photograph we see of Bon Scott there is something wicked and wonderfully, "Hey, this is rock and roll and I'm having a great time" about him, and that is the most powerful memory, and that is why he endures in our minds much more powerfully and much more potently than any one of say a hundred other tragic rock deaths that have just slipped by.[26]

Moving On

As powerful of a loss as Scott's death was, AC/DC was determined to keep moving forward. Songs for the next album had already been written. Scott had even practiced some of the songs that would be included on the next album when he sat in as the drummer on an impromptu jam session. But, without a singer, a huge hole in the band needed to be filled.

AC/DC's managers went through a long list of suggested lead singers. Most of them were already singers in their own bands. Some of them were quite successful and talented, but none of the lead singers they considered sounded right for AC/DC. Auditions were held in England, and an Australian singer named Allan Fryer caught the ears of two AC/DC managers. It was thought that the decision for the new lead singer had been decided, until a cassette tape showed up in the mail.[27] Stories say that a fan from Chicago, Illinois, sent a recording of a band called Geordie, from Northern England, to AC/DC managers. Brian Johnson was the lead singer on that tape. Legend also states that at one time, Scott himself had heard Brian Johnson sing and had mentioned that if AC/DC would ever need a singer that Johnson would do well. Angus once stated in an interview, "[Scott] was a big Little Richard fan—he believed that anyone singing rock 'n' roll would have to match

ONE MONTH AFTER BON SCOTT'S DEATH, AC/DC FOUND THEIR NEW LEAD SINGER—BRIAN JOHNSON (SECOND FROM LEFT) FROM THE BAND GEORDIE.

Little Richard. I remember [Scott] saying that Brian was a great rock 'n' roll singer in the Little Richard mold."[28]

Not long after they received the tape, AC/DC located Brian Johnson and asked him to join the band. Johnson accepted and was officially made part of AC/DC only one month after Scott's death. Some people may think his replacement was too sudden and that the band members should have taken longer to mourn Scott's death, but even Scott's father would disagree. At his son's funeral he mentioned to Malcolm, "You've got to find someone else, you know that."[29] Most people agree that Scott would have wanted the band to live on for as long as the fans would pay to buy records and concert tickets. Brian Johnson would prove to be the missing element that would help make fans scream for more from AC/DC for decades to come.

After practicing for a few weeks with Johnson, the band decided it was time to step out of England so they could focus on putting together their next album. They traveled to the Bahamas and rented a recording studio in Nassau. There the band could focus on their work without being distracted by the press or curious fans. Malcolm said, "It was the best place to do that album because there was nothing going on. We'd sit through the night . . . and work."[30]

While it may have been the perfect place to foster creativity, the atmosphere was also at times a bit too relaxing. For example, Johnson found it difficult to dig into his vocals. He enjoyed spending the first part of the day basking in the sun at the beach. When it was time to record, he would walk across the street to the recording studio, still wearing his swim trunks, and try to sing. In his relaxed state, he simply couldn't bring out the loud, gravelly sound in his voice that AC/DC was expecting. The solution was simple. Johnson went back to his hotel room and changed into his performance clothes. The problem was solved. Johnson's unique, screaming vocals exploded and the studio technicians captured it all on tape.[31]

Not only did Johnson take over Scott's role as a vocalist, but he was also asked to come up with lyrics. When asked about how he felt about writing for the album *Back in Black*, Johnson said, "There was no way out. The guys just said, 'would you try?' And luckily enough I came up with some useful lyrics. The lads had all the titles ready for us. "Back in Black" was particularly difficult because the boys were saying, 'We want this song in memory of [Scott] . . .' It was pretty tough, but I think we managed it pretty good, you know?"[32]

Success Continues

AC/DC certainly did "manage it pretty good." The album was hot and AC/DC fans were picking copies off of record store shelves at an incredible rate. In Los Angeles, California, the album sold 1.5 million copies.[33] Angus described the popularity of the album when he explained an incident that occurred soon after the album was released by saying, "I remember

AC/DC HAD A FRESH BEGINNING WITH BRIAN JOHNSON (LEFT, WEARING AN AC/DC SHIRT). THEIR ALBUM *BACK IN BLACK* IS ONE OF THE TOP-SELLING ROCK ALBUMS OF ALL TIME.

being in Australia six months later. We were going to go on holiday to Fiji or somewhere. This guy saw one of my nephews with the *Back in Black* jacket on, and he offered him five grand for it!"[34]

Back in Black slid up and down on the United States record chart for a full year. The album's highest ranking on the chart was number four and worldwide record sales reached more 41 million, placing it on the top ten list of top-selling rock albums of all time.[35] After the profound tragedy of losing

Scott, AC/DC was able to knock out a hugely successful album. There was now no question that AC/DC had made a solid choice when they asked Brian Johnson to join the band as the lead singer.

After *Back in Black*, AC/DC released *For Those About To Rock (We Salute You)*, which became the band's first album to rank number one in the United States. The impressive ranking won the band invitations to join both the 1984 Monsters of Rock Tour in England and the 1985 Rock in Rio, held in Brazil.

AC/DC continued to release albums about every two to three years, each adding at least one more classic song to the band's list of favorites. Their last album, *Stiff Upper Lip*, came out in the year 2000 and was paired with a successful concert tour. In 2002, AC/DC signed with a new record company, Sony.[36] Then, in 2008, AC/DC released a new album, *Black Ice*.

WHERE ARE THEY NOW?

There is no doubt AC/DC has come a long way. Looking back to their very first concert on New Year's Eve in 1973, the band was thrilled to have filled a small club in Sydney, Australia. Today, AC/DC, made up of members Brian Johnson, Phil Rudd, Cliff Williams, Angus Young, and Malcolm Young, can sell out arenas with the capacity to seat thousands of fans. In the 1970s, crowds were made up mostly of fans in their early twenties. Today, the range of ages of the audience is much broader. AC/DC draws fans young and old. Some gray-haired fans wear concert T-shirts older than their own children. These are the dedicated fans that have followed the band since it first started. Sometimes nostalgic parents bring their own children to AC/DC concerts in order to share with them an experience from their younger years. AC/DC concerts are not only for the older crowd. It seems that the band is sprouting a new generation of admirers. Teenagers also make up a great percentage of ticket sales. Robert Mancini, a reporter for MTV, described two fans that caught his eye at a 2003 concert held at the famous Roseland Ballroom in New York City. Mancini wrote: "There was the lanky teen boy clad in an oversized dress shirt, tie, and shorts (an homage to Angus' schoolboy get-up) pumping his fists and singing along. There was the teenage girl, sporting a tank top and a cap suspiciously like the one worn by Johnson, throwing her metal horns in the air and banging her head."[1]

It is no wonder AC/DC draws in a full spectrum of fans. Their music hasn't strayed from the blue-based rock that made them famous in the first place, and their stage shows are exciting and literally explosive. While AC/DC's equipment may have once fit in the back of a pickup truck, today it takes fourteen semitrailers to haul their elaborate stage set and special effects equipment.[2]

Modern Stage Shows

AC/DC has carried a wide range of props and equipment with them over the years. A giant bell announces the start of the song "Hells Bells" as its strong, almost eerie vibrations fill

AC/DC HAS USED MANY PROPS ON STAGE THROUGHOUT THEIR CAREER. A GIANT BELL ANNOUNCES THE START OF THE SONG "HELLS BELLS."

the stadium. The band has fired cannons onstage as a salute to the song "For Those About to Rock." A giant wrecking ball has flattened an enormous brick wall prop announcing the song "Ball Breaker." In 2000, a thirty-foot-tall statue made in the likeness of Angus provided a dramatic backdrop for the band.[3] The statue, which rose up from behind the drum kit, blew smoke from its mouth while its eyes glowed red.[4]

With set lists filled with basic rock and roll accompanied by elaborate stage effects, it is no wonder both old and young AC/DC fans stay true to their band for the long haul.

A massive fan base has its perks. High record and ticket sales have made life a little sweeter for the aging members of AC/DC as they now own fancy homes all over the world, are able to travel to exotic locations, and entertain themselves with expensive hobbies. Brian Johnson is a car enthusiast and spends as much time on the racetrack as he can. Surprisingly, his Florida home doesn't center around a musical theme. Johnson prefers to surround himself with cars. "My house is all cars, just cars. Cars, cars, more cars," said Johnson in an interview for No Nonsense AC/DC Webzine. Johnson doesn't just watch the cars circle the track. He likes to race himself. In the same interview, Johnson described his feelings about an upcoming race season when he said, "I can't wait . . . just the thrill of it, all the competition, crashing . . ." His enthusiasm for cars is as strong as a child's excitement for his or her next birthday.[5]

Famous but Not Flashy

For the most part, the members of AC/DC stay out of the public eye and lead relatively normal lives. It is difficult to find records of recent interviews with band members other than Brian Johnson and Angus Young. Johnson commented on the band members' private lifestyles when he said, "Because we keep a low profile we can walk around relatively unrecognized. And it's where we are living also. Phil lives in a small place in New Zealand, Malcolm lives in a small village, Angus is living in a small village. And Cliff lives in North Carolina, and I'm in Florida, but they are both small places. . . . So people know who you are, but it's an enjoyable situation. It must be hard to be a superstar; I could never handle that . . ."[6]

AC/DC'S BRIAN JOHNSON (LEFT) AND ANGUS YOUNG (RIGHT) PERFORM WITH STEVEN TYLER (CENTER) OF AEROSMITH DURING THE 18TH ANNUAL ROCK AND ROLL HALL OF FAME INDUCTION CEREMONY.

While AC/DC keeps a low profile when not on tour, they may be out of sight but they are certainly not forgotten. The band has been recognized for many achievements. In 2003, the band was graced with two important honors. AC/DC was inducted into the Rock and Roll Hall of Fame during the hall's eighteenth annual induction dinner on March 10, 2003. The band was welcomed to the list of honorees by the classic rock band Aerosmith.[7] Feeling a bit uncomfortable with the whole process, Brian Johnson said, "Yeah, we got on and did a few songs and watched people wearing the tuxes and evening gowns get up and go nuts. . . . It's very nice that so many bands have respect for us, but it does make me feel very uncomfortable. . . . We are always making sure that we keep that good feeling between us and the fans, and I think if they look at us as 'legends' that would be difficult. I'd rather have everyone just think of us as a good rock and roll band."[8] Soon after the induction into the hall, AC/DC was honored with another award. This time the award recognized their contribution to Australian music. The Ted Albert Award for Outstanding Service to Australian Music was awarded to Angus, Malcolm, and Scott on May 20, 2003. Because the APRA awards are given to songwriters, only Angus, Malcolm, and Scott were recognized and not the entire band. Malcolm spoke for the group as he accepted the award. Though long after Scott's death, Malcolm made sure his old friend as well as the entire band were remembered when he said, "On behalf of AC/DC and Bon Scott, especially Bon as he's a big part of this, we're proud of the honour of receiving this award."[9] The award was particularly appropriate for the boys from AC/DC as the band's first album, *High Voltage*, was signed under the label Albert Records, the company founded by Ted Albert, the same man for whom the award was created.[10]

Giving Back

While AC/DC has had honors given to them, the members of the band also take time to give back to others. AC/DC has been involved with several charity concerts. In 2003, AC/DC teamed up with the Rolling Stones and several other popular artists as they worked to raise funds for disease relief during the Rolling Stones Toronto SARS Concert. An estimated four hundred thousand people filled Downsview Park, Toronto. The concert raised more than $7 million to help Toronto and Canada get back on track after being afflicted with the hardships of two diseases, SARS and mad cow disease.[11]

Brian Johnson and Cliff Williams, the two members of AC/DC who live in the United States, took action soon after a round of devastating hurricanes hit Florida in 2005. On December 15, 2005, Johnson and Williams, along with several popular performers such as Robin Zander from Cheap Trick and Eddie Money, performed under the organization of the John Entwistle Foundation, a charitable organization that puts together benefit concerts, to help raise money to help rebuild communities in Florida that were destroyed by hurricanes.[12]

Johnson and Williams were involved in another Entwistle event called Classic Rock Cares. During the summer of 2007, the two AC/DC members joined classic rockers from Grand Funk Railroad and Deep Purple as they raised money to help provide musical instruments and music lessons for underprivileged children. The tour covered seven cities including Chicago; Ft. Meyers, Florida; and Las Vegas. Johnson and Williams performed both classic AC/DC tunes as well as some new songs. The song "Chain Gang on the Road" was written specifically for the charity event and proved to fans that Johnson and Williams are still able to put out new, exciting material.[13]

The hint of new material was very exciting to AC/DC fans. The band hadn't put out a new album for over ten years. On October 20, 2008, the dry spell came to a screeching halt when AC/DC released *Black Ice*. The album fed the public's hunger for new music and the screaming vocals of Johnson did not disappoint. Fans snatched up copies of *Black Ice* from small pop-up stores selling exclusive AC/DC merchandise on the streets of cities New York and Los Angeles. For those fans not lucky enough to have access to one of these temporary retail outlets, a trip to Wal-Mart or Sam's Club was a must as these stores are the only outlets in the United States licensed to sell the hot new album. In just two weeks *Black Ice* sold over one million copies and had topped the rock charts in over twenty-nine countries, including the United States.

AC/DC Sometimes Seen in Unusual Places

AC/DC and its music often pop up in unexpected places. The March 18, 2000, episode of *Saturday Night Live*, a late-night comedy show, touted AC/DC as the musical guest for the evening where they played the songs "Stiff Upper Lip" and "You Shook Me All Night Long" to a crowd of adoring and excited fans.[14]

Besides making appearances on popular television shows, Angus made his mark on the guitar world when he received an honored salute from the Gibson Guitar Company. Angus has played Gibson guitars throughout his career. His spectacular talent did not go unnoticed by the people at Gibson when they crafted a signature SG model guitar in Angus's name.[15]

While Angus may have had a guitar made in his name-sake, the entire band was honored when the city of Melbourne, Australia, decided to name a street after the band. AC/DC Lane is marked by a large, blue and white street sign complete with a bolt of lightning splitting down the center. City council members stated that the street was a perfect fit as it ran through the heart of the city's bar and rock district. Council member Kimberley Kitching said, "AC/DC is a world-renowned

THE CITY OF MELBOURNE, AUSTRALIA, HONORED THE
BAND BY NAMING A STREET AFTER IT—AC/DC LANE.

band and they wrote most of their first album in Melbourne
. . . we should honour that."[16]

While finding an Angus Young signature guitar, or driving
down a street marked with the letters AC/DC are quirky
examples of fame used in marketing, seeing AC/DC in the
aisles of a toy store may be a complete surprise to many. With
a list of songs titles that make most adults cringe, one may
wonder how the band could ever end up in the children's
department of any store. As funny as it may seem, the like-
nesses of Brian Johnson and Angus Young have been turned

into plastic dolls, or as some may prefer to say, action figures. The Brian doll stands with bulging biceps, fists clenched, holding a microphone while gritting his teeth, just as the real artist does during performances. The Angus doll is shirtless, wearing the trademark long shorts with crew socks and running shoes. Its body is hunched over a guitar while the molded plastic hair is tousled as though the gyrating performer was frozen in the middle of a wild guitar solo. While the dolls were most likely created to satisfy cravings of AC/DC collectors, the idea of children playing "rock star" with miniature models of Johnson and Angus is quite comical.[17]

While Johnson and Angus did not come up with the idea of turning themselves into action figures, their actions and hard work, along with the other members of AC/DC, sent the band soaring to the top. Older brother Malcolm put the wheels in motion as his vision for a new rock band prompted him to place an ad in the newspaper asking for new players. Sister Margaret helped add spice to her brother's idea when she helped the band come up with their name and again when she took Angus out of his superhero costume and placed him in his school uniform. The boys took off from there, giving everything they had to fulfill their strong desire to do nothing more than play some gritty, ear-blasting rock and roll. Since the early days, AC/DC has not strayed from their idea of what rock and roll should be—simple, loud, and fun—and their fans are thankful for that. AC/DC has stood the test of time without giving in to the temptation of experimentation at the risk of losing its identity as a band.

AC/DC is a band that has come full circle. Over thirty years ago, the band was begging for fans; now, fans are begging for more AC/DC. Their demands have not gone unheard. With copies of *Black Ice* in hand, excited fans lined up around stadiums, waiting to catch a glimpse of their favorite band. On October 28, 2008, in Wilkes-Barre, Pennsylvania, AC/DC began a word tour that is scheduled to keep the band on the road through April 2009.

AC/DC is definitely an example of a band that started from the bottom—practicing guitar after school in their bedrooms and taking the stage in superhero costumes with a band named for the label on their sister's sewing machine. They crawled the long way to the top with a long list of platinum albums, and they have the ability to fill stadiums with thousands of fans, where they have managed to gain the status of being one of the greatest classic rock bands that ever played.

TIMELINE

1973—December 31: AC/DC debuts at Chequers Club in Sydney, Australia.

1974—Bon Scott joins the band. First album, *High Voltage* (Australian version), is recorded.

1975—Phil Rudd and Mark Evans join the band. *High Voltage* receives triple-gold.

1976—*High Voltage* is released in United States. The Lock Up Your Daughters tour is launched in the United Kingdom.

1977—AC/DC appears on the television show *Countdown*. The band signs with Atlantic Records. Cliff Williams replaces Mark Evans as bass guitar player.

1978—AC/DC tours worldwide.

1980—Bon Scott dies on February 19. Brian Johnson joins as new lead singer.

1981—AC/DC plays in Japan for the first time.

1982—AC/DC takes a break from touring.

1984—The band headlines Monsters of Rock tour in Europe.

1985—AC/DC kicks off North American tour.

1986—The band shoots music videos for "Who Made Who" and "You Shook Me All Night Long."

1987—The band focuses on recording new music.

1991—AC/DC headlines Monsters of Rock tour for the third time. The band also headlines Rock Around the Bloc festival in Moscow, Russia.

1994—Phil Rudd rejoins band after an eleven-year absence. AC/DC pairs with a new label, East/West Records.

1995—The band hits a milestone of selling more than 80 million albums worldwide.

1996—The band receives a Silver Clef Award.

1998—A Lifetime Achievement award is received from *Kerrang!* magazine.

1999—The Diamond Award is received after 10 million *Back in Black* records are sold.

2000—AC/DC appears on an MTV television show for the first time in twenty-three years. The band is added to Hollywood's Rock Walk.

2002—AC/DC is voted into the Rock and Roll Hall of Fame. The band signs with Epic Records.

2003—AC/DC plays at an intimate concert hall, Roseland Ballroom, in New York City; AC/DC joins the Rolling Stones in the the group's Toronto SARS benefit concert.

2005—Brian Johnson and Cliff Williams play a benefit concert for hurricane victims.

2007—Brian Johnson and Cliff Williams join other classic rock icons in the Classic Rock Cares concert to raise money for music education for underprivileged children.

2008—AC/DC releases the album *Black Ice* in October; the band's first new album in over ten years. That same month the band hit the road for the worldwide Black Ice tour.

2009—Black Ice tour continues through April.

DISCOGRAPHY

1975 *High Voltage (Australia)*

1976 *T.N.T.*

High Voltage

Dirty Deeds Done Dirt Cheap (Australia)

Dirty Deeds Done Dirt Cheap

1977 *Let There Be Rock (Australia)*

Let There Be Rock

1978 *Powerage*

If You Want Blood

1979 *Highway to Hell*

1980 *Back in Black*

1981 *For Those About to Rock*

1983 *Flick of the Switch*

1984 *'74 Jailbreak*

1985 *Fly on the Wall*

1986 *Who Made Who*

1988 *Blow Up Your Video*

1990 *The Razors Edge*

1992 *Live*

Live: Special Collector's Edition 2 CD Set

1995 *Ballbreaker*

1997 *Live from the Atlantic Studios*

Volts

2000 *Stiff Upper Lip*

2008 *Black Ice*

CONCERT TOURS

1975 High Voltage Tour (Australia); T.N.T. Tour (Australia)

1976 T.N.T Tour (Australia); High Voltage Tour (Europe)

1977 Let There Be Rock Tour

1978 Powerage Tour

1978–1979 If You Want Blood Tour

1979–1980 Highway to Hell World Tour

1980–1981 Back in Black World Tour

1981–1982 For Those About to Rock World Tour

1983–1984 Flick of the Switch Tour

1985–1986 Fly on the Wall World Tour

1986 Who Made Who American Tour

1988 Blow Up Your Video World Tour

1990–1991 The Razors Edge World Tour

1996 Ballbreaker World Tour

2000–2001 Stiff Upper Lip World Tour

2003 Extraordinary Concerts

2008–2009 Black Ice World Tour

GLOSSARY

amplifier—A piece of electronic equipment into which electric or electronic instruments are plugged to make their sound louder.

authenticity—The quality of being real, genuine, or pure.

blue-collar—A slang term used to refer to a person who performs manual or industrial labor.

drongo—Australian slang used to describe a person as stupid or a total idiot.

epileptic—Reference to a neurological condition that may cause sudden attacks of body spasms and loss of consciousness.

farmhand—One who works on a farm doing manual labor.

gimmick—A unique idea, trick, or gadget used to attract attention or interest.

immigrating—The act of moving from one country to another with the intent of living in the new country permanently.

locals—A slang term used to identify persons who are native to a certain country, state, or city.

mad cow disease—A fatal brain disease afflicting cattle that can be passed to humans who eat infected meat.

migrant hostel—An inexpensive, supervised lodge used mostly by travelers or students.

overpopulation—A situation that occurs when the amount of people in a given area exhausts the resources available.

pandemonium—A wild uproar of noise, chaos, and excitement.

petrol—British term for gasoline.

SARS—Severe acute respiratory syndrome. Highly contagious type of pneumonia.

sack—A slang term used to describe the act of being fired or losing one's job.

siphoning—The act of using suction to pull liquid through a tube to transfer it from one container to another. Also refers to the act of stealing gas from a parked vehicle using this method.

spiked—A slang term that refers to a drink to which either a drug or alcohol has been added.

vile—Evil, immoral, disgusting, or repulsive.

CHAPTER NOTES

Chapter 1. A New Year, a New Band

1. Martin Huxley, *AC/DC: The World's Heaviest Rock* (New York: St. Martin's Griffin, 1996), p. 19.

2. Paul Stenning, *Two Sides to Every Glory: AC/DC The Complete Biography* (New Malden, Surrey, U.K.: Chrome Dreams, 2005), p. 25.

3. Clinton Walker, *Highway to Hell: The Life & Times of AC/DC Legend Bon Scott* (Portland, Oreg.: Verse Chorus Press, 2001), p. 128.

4. Susan Masino, *Let There Be Rock: The Story of AC/DC* (New York: Omnibus Press, 2006), p. 10.

5. Murray Engleheart, *AC/DC: Maximum Rock & Roll* (New York: HarperCollins, 2006), p. 58.

6. Masino, p. 8.

7. Malcolm Dome, *AC/DC* (New York: Proteus Books, 1982), p. 18.

8. Stenning, p. 28.

9. Dome, p. 20.

10. Ibid., p. 18.

11. Ibid.

12. Ibid.

Chapter 2. Band of Brothers

1. Paul Stenning, *Two Sides to Every Glory:*

AC/DC the Complete Biography (New Malden, Surrey, U.K.: Chrome Dreams, 2005), p. 13.

2. Ibid.

3. Susan Masino, *Let There Be Rock: The Story of AC/DC* (New York: Omnibus Press, 2006), p. 1.

4. Ibid.

5. Stenning, pp. 15–16.

6. Malcolm Dome, *AC/DC* (New York: Proteus Books, 1982), p. 14.

7. Stenning, p. 19.

8. Masino, p. 2.

9. Ibid., p. 4.

10. Stenning, pp. 19–20.

11. Masino, p. 4.

12. Stenning, p. 22.

13. Ibid., p. 23.

14. Masino, p. 7.

15. Kerrang!, *AC/DC: The Definitive History*, ed. Malcolm Dome (London: Virgin Books Ltd., 2002), p. 26.

16. Clinton Walker, *Highway to Hell: The Life & Times of AC/DC Legend Bon Scott* (Portland, Oreg.: Verse Chorus Press, 2001), pp. 29–30.

17. Masino, p. 18.

18. Ibid.

19. Walker, p. 32.

20. Murray Engleheart, *AC/DC: Maximum Rock & Roll* (New York: HarperCollins, 2006), p. 66.

21. Ibid.

22. Masino, p. 19.

23. Martin Huxley, *AC/DC: The World's Heaviest Rock* (New York: St. Martin's Griffin, 1996), p. 27.

24. Ibid.

25. Ibid.

26. Walker, pp. 40–41.

27. Ibid., p. 44.

28. Ibid.

29. Huxley, p. 28.

30. Walker, p. 48.

31. Ibid., p. 49.

32. Masino, p. 21.

33. Walker, p. 55.

34. Huxley, p. 31.

35. Ibid.

36. Author unknown, "Brian Johnson Biography," AOL Music, n.d., <http://www.music.aol.com/artist/brian-johnson/biography/100023> (June 21, 2007).

37. Masino, p. 30.

38. Ibid.

39. Huxley, p. 197.

40. Engleheart, p. 197.

41. Author unknown, "The Beatles," Rock and Roll Hall of Fame, 1988, <http://www.rockhall.com/inductee/the-beatles> (November 29, 2007).

42. Engleheart, p. 198.

43. Stenning, p. 75.

44. Masino, p. 57.

Chapter 3. A Spark Explodes

1. Paul Stenning, *Two Sides to Every Glory: AC/DC The Complete Biography* (New Malden, Surrey, U.K.: Chrome Dreams, 2005), p. 24.

2. "Dave Evans Podcast Interview," Hard Rock Hideout, n.d., <http://hardrockhideout.files.wordpress.com/2007/06/hardrockhideout-daveevansinterview.mp3> (July 9, 2007).

3. Author unknown, "Interview: Dave Evans, Part 1," No Nonsense AC/DC Webzine, August 8, 1999, <http://www.kolumbus.fi/nononsense/dave1.htm> (April 3, 2007).

4. Stenning, p. 24.

5. Ibid.

6. Ibid.

7. Ibid.

8. Ibid.

9. Malcolm Dome, *AC/DC* (New York: Proteus Books, 1982), p. 16.

10. Author unknown, "Interview: Dave Evans, Part 1," No Nonsense AC/DC Webzine, August 8, 1999, <http://www.kolumbus.fi/nononsense/dave1.htm> (April 3, 2007).

11. Murray Engleheart, *AC/DC: Maximum Rock & Roll* (New York: HarperCollins, 2006), p. 51.

12. Author unknown, "Interview: Dave Evans, Part 1," No Nonsense AC/DC Webzine, August 8,

1999, <http://www.kolumbus.fi/nononsense/dave1.htm> (April 3, 2007).

13. Stenning, p. 26.

14. "Selfdrive from Adelaide to Perth," Pacific Island Travel, n.d., <http://www.pacificislandtravel.com/australia/selfdrives/scoverlander_adlper.html> (November 29, 2007).

15. Kerrang!, *AC/DC: The Definitive History*, ed. Malcolm Dome (London: Virgin Books Ltd., 2002), p. 25.

16. Stenning, p. 46.

17. Martin Huxley, *AC/DC: The World's Heaviest Rock* (New York: St. Martin's Griffin, 1996), p. 43.

18. Clinton Walker, *Highway to Hell: The Life & Times of AC/DC Legend Bon Scott* (Portland, Oreg.: Verse Chorus Press, 2001), p. 131.

19. Ibid., p. 133.

20. Stenning, p. 32.

21. Kerrang!, p. 30.

22. AC/DC, *High Voltage*, Australia: Albert Records, 1974.

23. Stenning, p. 53.

24. Ibid., p. 54.

25. Engleheart, p. 111.

26. Susan Masino, *Let There Be Rock: The Story of AC/DC* (New York: Omnibus Press, 2006), p. 32.

27. Ibid., p. 31.

28. Masino, p. 36.

29. Engleheart, p. 457.

30. Stenning, p. 60.

Chapter 4. The World Around AC/DC

1. Valerie Woodring Goertzen, "Blues," *World Book Encyclopedia*, version 6.0 (Chicago: World Book, Inc., 2001).

2. Author unknown, "It's a Long John: Traditional African-American Work Songs," *History Matters: The U.S. Survey Course on the Web*, n.d., <http://historymatters.gmu.edu/d/5758> (June 6, 2007).

3. Author unknown, "Blues Instruments," Blues Project, n.d., <http://www.bluesproject.org/Instruments/Instrument.htm> (June 8, 2007).

4. Author unknown, "Blues Vocabulary," Blues Project, n.d., <http://www.bluesproject.org/Bluesproject/Blues%20Vocabulary.htm> (June 8, 2007).

5. Francis Davis, *The History of the Blues: The Roots, the Music, the People: From Charley Patton to Robert Cray* (New York: Hyperion, 1995), p. 44.

6. Ibid., p. 209.

7. Don McLeese, "Rock and Roll Music," *World Book Encyclopedia*, version 6.0 (Chicago: World Book, Inc., 2001), pp. 1–9.

8. Robert Palmer, *Rock & Roll: An Unruly History* (New York: Harmony Books, 1995), p. 40.

9. Ibid., p. 43.

10. Susan Masino, *Let There Be Rock: The Story of AC/DC* (New York: Omnibus Press, 2006), pp. 14–15.

11. Clinton Walker, *Highway to Hell: The Life & Times of AC/DC Legend Bon Scott* (Portland, Oreg.: Verse Chorus Press, 2001), p. 13.

12. Author unknown, "1970s: The Me Decade," Thompson Gale, n.d., <http://www.galegroup.com/pdf/samples/sp656755.pdf> (July 7, 2007).

13. Ibid.

14. Engleheart, p. 357.

15. Ibid., p. 366.

Chapter 5. Life After Scott

1. Kerrang!, *AC/DC: The Definitive History*, ed. Malcolm Dome (London: Virgin Books Ltd., 2002), pp. 32, 37.

2. Ibid., p. 38.

3. Susan Masino, *Let There Be Rock: The Story of AC/DC* (New York: Omnibus Press, 2006), p. 61.

4. Ibid., pp. 64, 66.

5. Ibid., p. 67.

6. Clinton Walker, *Highway to Hell: The Life & Times of AC/DC Legend Bon Scott* (Portland, Oreg.: Verse Chorus Press, 2001), p. 173.

7. Ibid., p. 197.

8. Ibid.

9. Ibid., pp. 232–233.

10. Ibid., p. 276.

11. Murray Engleheart, *AC/DC: Maximum Rock & Roll* (New York: HarperCollins, 2006), p. 291.

12. Ibid.

13. Walker, p. 275.

14. Martin Huxley, *AC/DC: The World's Heaviest Rock* (New York: St. Martin's Griffin, 1996), p. 108.

15. Engleheart, pp. 291–292.

16. Walker, p. 277.

17. Huxley, p. 108.

18. Engleheart, p. 292.

19. Ibid.

20. Walker, p. 277.

21. Author unknown, "Copy of Scott's Death Certificate," *Crabsody in Blue*, <http://www.crabsodyinblue.com/certificatedeces.gif> (June 18, 2007).

22. Paul Stenning, *Two Sides to Every Glory: AC/DC The Complete Biography* (New Malden, Surrey, U.K.: Chrome Dreams, 2005), p. 103.

23. Ibid.

24. Ibid.

25. Masino, p. 111.

26. Denise Knight, "20th Anniversary of Bon Scott's Death This Weekend," *The World Today Archive*, 2000, <http://www.abc.net.au/worldtoday/stories/s101535.htm> (June 18, 2007).

27. Huxley, pp. 116–117.

28. Masino, p. 112.

29. Walker, p. 291.

30. Masino, p. 114.

31. Ibid., p. 116.

32. Author unknown, "Interview With Brian Johnson: Breaking Training," *VH1 Ultimate Albums*, n.d., <http://www.vh1.com/shows/dyn/ultimate_albums/67291/episode_interviews_int.jhtml?start=2> (June 20, 2007).

33. Author unknown, "Interview With Angus Young: If You Want Crabs (You've Got 'Em)," *VH1 Ultimate Albums*, n.d., <http://www.vh1.com/shows/dyn/ultimate_albums/67291/episode_interviews_int.jhtml?start=1> (June 20, 2007).

34. Ibid.

35. Author unknown, "Induction Year: 2003, Category: Performer," *Rock and Roll Hall of Fame and Museum*, 2003, <http://www.rockhall.com/inductee/ac-dc> (June 21, 2007).

36. Ibid.

Chapter 6. Where Are They Now?

1. Robert Mancini, "AC/DC Take Manhattan; Deliver Their Only U.S. Show for 2003," *MTV News*, March 12, 2003, <http://www.mtv.com/news/articles/1470496/20030312/acdc.jhtml> (June 26, 2007).

2. "AC/DC 60 Minutes (Australia) Interview,"

1996, <http://www.leechvideo.com/video/view2647246.html> (July 26, 2007).

3. Paul Robicheau, "AC/DC Show Still Ain't a Bad Place to Be," *Rolling Stone News*, August 10, 2000, <http://www.rollingstone.com/news/story/5924510/acdc_show_still_aint_a_bad_place_to_be/print> (June 26, 2007).

4. Paul M. Roy, "AC/DC: Stiff Upper Lip Live," *Concert Reviews*, June 2004, <http://www.concertdvdreviews.com/Reviews/ACDC_Stiff.htm> (June 26, 2007).

5. Author unknown, "Brian Johnson Interview," *No Nonsense AC/DC Webzine*, June 27, 2001, <http://www.kolumbus.fi/nononsense/brian.htm> (June 28, 2007).

6. Paul Stenning, *Two Sides to Every Glory: AC/DC The Complete Biography* (New Malden, Surrey, U.K.: Chrome Dreams, 2005), p. 237.

7. Author unknown, "Induction Year: 2003," *Rock and Roll Hall of Fame*, March 2003, <http://www.rockhall.com/inductee/ac-dc> (June 28, 2007).

8. Stenning, p. 216.

9. Author unknown, "2003 APRA Music Award Winners Announced," *APRA/AMCOS* Music Awards, 2003, <http://www.apra.com.au/awards/music/media_releases/03-music_award_winners_announced.asp> (June 28, 2007).

10. Paul Cashmere, "Malcolm Thanks Bon for

AC/DC Award," *Undercover Music News*, May 20, 2003, <http://www.undercover.com.au/news/2003/ 20030520_acdc.html> (June 29, 2007).

11. Author unknown, "Stones, AC/DC rock Canadian SARS concert," July 31, 2003, <http:// www.abc.net.au/news/stories/2003/07/31/914171.htm> (April 11, 2008).

12. Author unknown, "K-Rock For Relief 2," *Crabsody in Blue*, n.d., <http://www.crabsodyinblue. com/acdckrockforrelif2005.htm> (July 26, 2007).

13. Author unknown, "Classic Rock Cares," *The John Entwistle Foundation*, 2007, <http://www. johnentwistle.org/crc/crc.html> (June 25, 2007).

14. Author unknown, "Saturday Night Live Episode #25.15," *Saturday Night Live Transcripts*, March 2000, <http://snltranscripts.jt.org/99/99o. phtml> (June 25, 2007).

15. Author unknown, "Gibson Salutes Angus Young," *Gibson Guitar: Backstage Pass*, n.d., <http:// www.gibson.com/backstage%20Pass/200705/ angus%20young/> (June 26, 2007).

16. Patrick Donovan and Martin Boulton, "Mayor Thunderstruck With AC/DC," *The Age*, July 8, 2004, <http://www.theage.com/articles/2004/07/07/ 1089000225625.html> (June 26, 2007).

17. Author unknown, "The Perfect Toy . . . For Those About to Rock," *Stuck in the '80s*, June 28, 2007, <http://blogs.tampabay.com/80s/2007/06/ please-add-this.html> (June 29, 2007).

FURTHER READING

Books

Brasch, Nicolas. *Pop and Rock Music.* North Mankato, Minn.: Smart Apple Media, 2004.

Gilmour, Sarah. *The 70s: Punks, Glam Rockers, and New Romantics.* Milwaukee, Wisc.: Gareth Stevens Pub., 2000.

Hayes, Malcolm. *1970s: Turbulent Times.* Milwaukee, Wisc.: Gareth Stevens Pub., 2002.

Masino, Susan. *The Story of AC/DC.* London: Omnibus Press, 2006.

Schaefer, A.R. *Forming a Band.* Mankato, Minn.: Capstone High-Interest Books, 2004.

Schlesinger, Ethan. *AC/DC.* Broomall, Penn.: Mason Crest Publishers, 2007.

Stenning, Paul. *AC/DC: Two Sides to Every Glory: The Complete Biography.* London: Chrome Dreams, 2007.

Internet Addresses

AC/DC
<http://www.mtv.com/music/artist/acdc/artist.jhtml>

AC/DC: Electric Shock
<http://www.ac-dc.net/>

INDEX